Gita

Stories

Persons interested in the purchasing or the distributing of this book may contact the publisher.

Published in 2021 by
Touchstone Media
Shri Krishna Sharnam Block B Flat 206
Vrindavan, Mathura Dist., 281221, UP, INDIA
Email: sales@touchstonemedia.com
www.touchstonemedia.com

ISBN: 978-81-937276-3-8

TOUCHSTONE
M E D I A
Matter for the Soul

Gita Stories

Spoken by Lord Shiva
to Parvati

Retold & Illustrated
by
Ananta Shakti Das

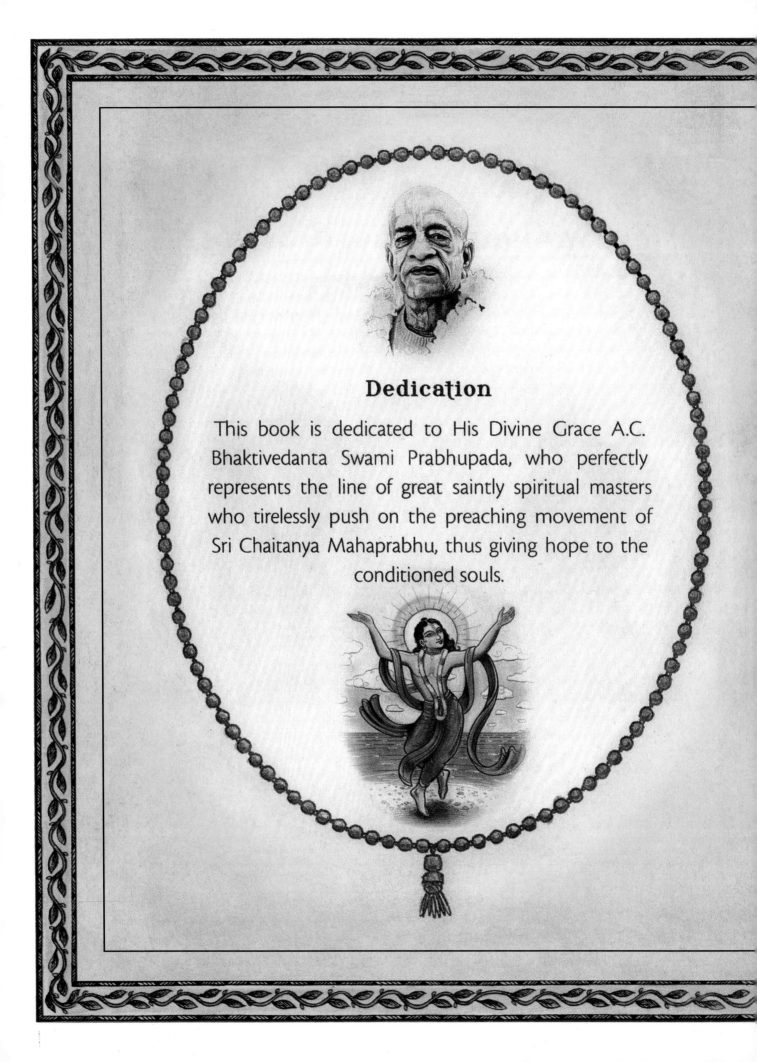

Dedication

This book is dedicated to His Divine Grace A.C. Bhaktivedanta Swami Prabhupada, who perfectly represents the line of great saintly spiritual masters who tirelessly push on the preaching movement of Sri Chaitanya Mahaprabhu, thus giving hope to the conditioned souls.

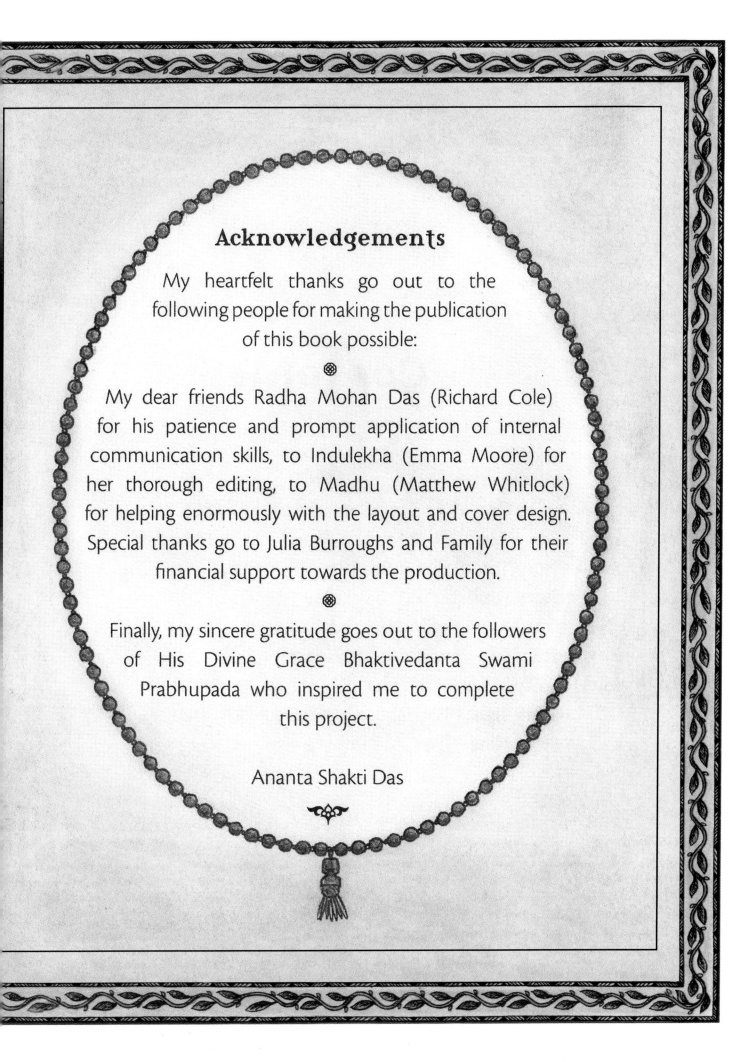

Acknowledgements

My heartfelt thanks go out to the
following people for making the publication
of this book possible:

❂

My dear friends Radha Mohan Das (Richard Cole)
for his patience and prompt application of internal
communication skills, to Indulekha (Emma Moore) for
her thorough editing, to Madhu (Matthew Whitlock)
for helping enormously with the layout and cover design.
Special thanks go to Julia Burroughs and Family for their
financial support towards the production.

❂

Finally, my sincere gratitude goes out to the followers
of His Divine Grace Bhaktivedanta Swami
Prabhupada who inspired me to complete
this project.

Ananta Shakti Das

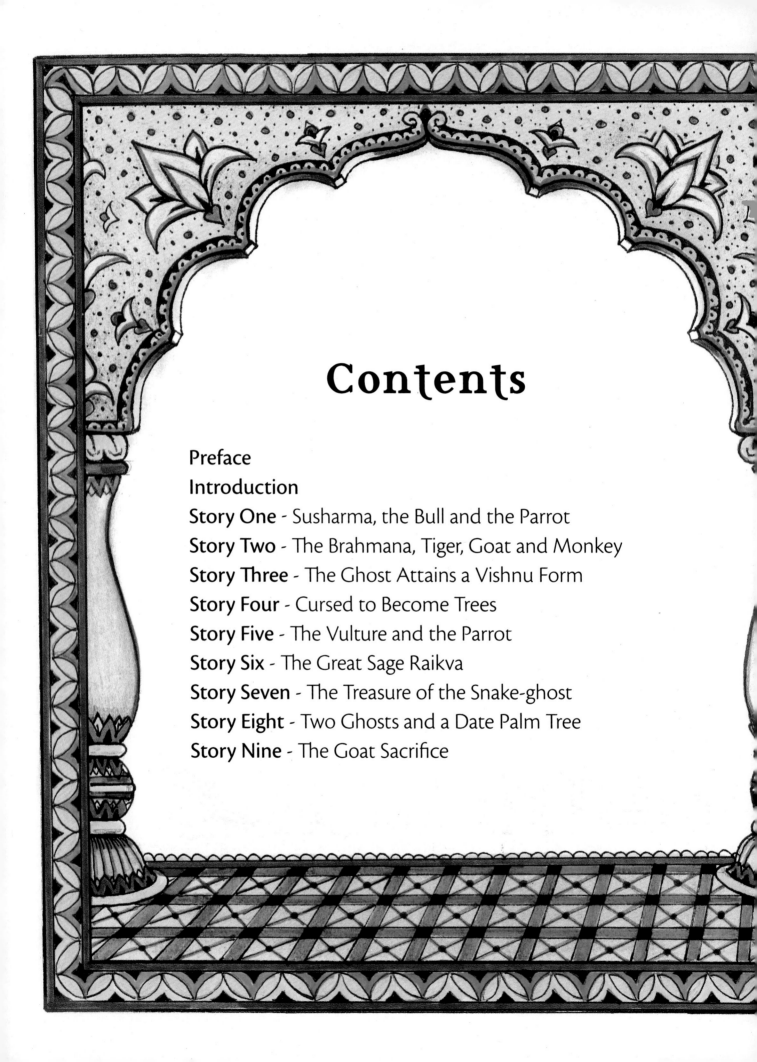

Contents

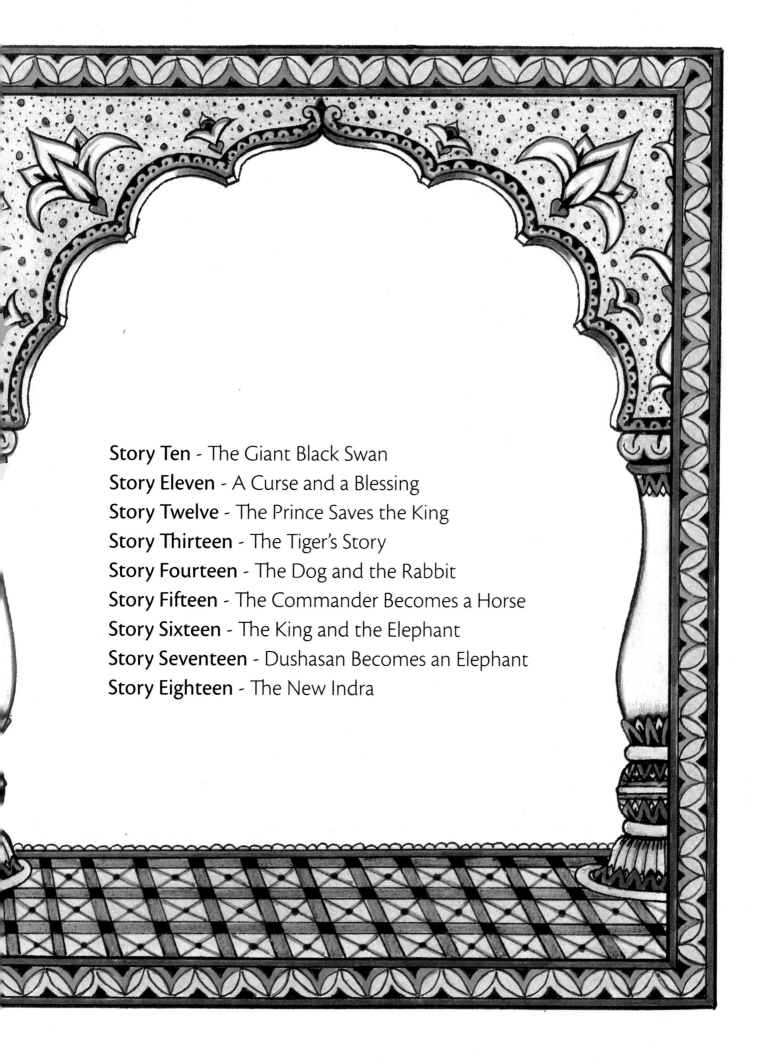

Shiva glorifies Vishnu

The Goddess Parvati enquired from Lord Shiva, "My dear Lord Shiva, you possess all spiritual knowledge and have explained to me so many truths about Shri Krishna, the Supreme Lord. Now, a great desire has arisen in me to hear more of the Lord's glories, especially in regard to His instructions to His dear friend Arjuna. I am sure that by hearing something about that sacred conversation, my devotion to the Supreme Lord will increase."

Lord Shiva replied, "As you well know, Lord Krishna, as the original creator, is also known as Lord Vishnu and has a body which is the hue of dark rain clouds. He lies upon the soft coils of Ananta-Sesha, the thousand-headed celestial serpent. To that Lord Vishnu who possesses unlimited glories, I constantly offer worship."

"My dear Parvati, long ago, after Lord Vishnu killed the demon Mura, He took rest on Ananta-Sesha. During that time, the goddess of fortune, Lakshmi, approached Him. Observing His peaceful divine form and the smiling expression on His face Lakshmi inquired "My dear Lord, although You have the responsibility of controlling and maintaining all of the created universes, I see that you are sleeping happily on this ocean of milk, how can this be?"

Lord Vishnu opened His lotus-shaped eyes and replied "My dear Lakshmi, I may appear to be sleeping but actually I am enjoying the wonderful play of my divine energies. It is by means of my unlimited power that I control all things. Yet at the same time I remain aloof and untouched by all these created worlds. By thinking about My divine activities, great yogis and devotees free themselves from birth and death and enter into spiritual life which is eternal and free from all suffering."

"My mystical energies which entrap fallen souls in these worlds of birth and death are difficult to overcome. However, for those who develop pure intelligence and offer loving service unto Me, the path of real freedom is open. Knowledge of this science is fully explained in the sacred words of *Bhagavad-gita*."

Lakshmi said, "My Lord, please explain how Your words in the *Bhagavad-gita* bring one to an understanding of Your spiritual nature?"

Lord Vishnu replied "I will explain this to you, Devi, but please understand, this *Bhagavad-gita* is My very self. My five heads appear as the first five chapters, My ten arms are the following ten chapters, My stomach is the sixteenth chapter and My two lotus feet are the last two chapters. In this way the Deity of *Bhagavad-gita* can be understood. This *Bhagavad-gita* destroys all sins and an intelligent person who daily recites one chapter, one verse, half a verse or even quarter of a verse will achieve all perfection." Thus begins the Gita-Mahatmya."

The Demon of Doubt

(Introductory Story)

Once upon a time there was a poor *brahmana*, who lived with his wife in a small cottage. Every day he would devotedly read the *Bhagavad-gita* before going out to beg alms. One day, he was studying the ninth chapter and came to this verse:

ananyas cintayanto mam
ye janah paryupasate
tesam nityabhiyuktanam
yoga-kseman vahamya aham

Translation – "Those who always worship Me with exclusive devotion, meditating on My transcendental form – to them I carry what they lack and I preserve what they have."

The demon of doubt suddenly entered the *brahmana's* mind and he seriously questioned the direct meaning of the verse. "Bhagavan, the Supreme Lord, personally carries and delivers the needs of His devotees?"

"How can that be so? I can understand that he empowers others to fulfil the needs of his devotees, but to do that personally doesn't sound right to me. This must be a mistake." After much careful thought, the *brahmana* took a pen and ink and scratched out the words he considered to be wrong. He then left his house.

On that day, wherever the *brahmana* went and whichever door he knocked upon, he was not offered a grain of rice or even a pinch of salt. Everybody had a good reason for refusing him. It seemed as though fate was against him and he was meant to go hungry.

In the meantime, whilst the *brahmana* was out, hearing a knock at the door, his wife opened it. To her surprise a beautiful boy was standing there with a heavy load on his back.

The boy said "Dear mother, your husband is my guru, and he has sent these foodstuffs for you." The *brahmana's* wife replied, "I think there must be some mistake; my husband has no disciples - you must have the wrong address." The boy replied by saying her husband's name and then put the load down at her feet.

As he did this she noticed red marks across the boy's back and enquired, "My dear boy, what happened to your back, please tell me?"

The boy replied "Your husband disagreed with something I said, so he punished me."

The *brahmana's* wife was both shocked and puzzled to hear such a thing, "Oh, this is terrible!" she said, "Come in and rest and I will cook something for you to eat."

With that, she picked up the bag of oil, rice, *dhal* and vegetables and went inside, astonished at how unkind her husband had become.

At the end of a fruitless day the *brahmana* returned home in a gloomy mood, only to be greeted by his furious wife.

"How dare you have a secret disciple and treat him so cruelly" she scolded, waving a rolling pin in the air.

"There are marks all over his back where you beat him simply because you disagreed with something he said. Come, see for yourself." The young boy however, had mysteriously disappeared. Although they looked everywhere, the couple were unable to find him.

Later, after his evening meal, the *brahmana* opened the *Bhagavad-gita* on the same page where he had finished his studies that morning. Much to his surprise, he saw that the verse he had disagreed with was unmarked because the crossing out lines had disappeared. Immediately, he realized his mistake and began to lament bitterly. "How stupid of me to doubt the words of Lord

Krishna which are not different from His very self. He came as my own disciple, in the form of that young boy, simply to teach me a lesson. He felt my marks as if I were striking His back. My good wife was fortunate enough to have His *darshan*, but due to lack of faith, I missed Him. I am most unfortunate."

The *brahmana* buried his head in his hands and wept.

In this way, that brahmana became an object of instruction for all of us who read the sacred words of the *Bhagavad-gita*. We should read it not as it could have been or should have been written according to our own thinking, but in the way Lord Krishna Himself spoke it - the *Bhagavad-gita* as it is and as it will always be, perfect and complete!"

Susharma, the Bull and the Parrot

The Goddess Lakshmi enquired from Lord Vishnu "My dear Lord, in regards to the glories of *Bhagavad-gita*, I have heard you mention the name of a great devotee - Susharma. Please tell me, which *varna*, or social class, did he belong to? What position did he achieve due to his devotion to You?" Lord Vishnu replied "My dear Lakshmi, although Susharma was born in a *brahmana* family they were nonetheless very ignorant people. Susharma was cruel by nature. He would never give in charity, receive guests and he never chanted My names. Truthfully speaking, nothing good could be said of him. Susharma passed his life

by selling leaf plates for money, which he wasted on wine and meat.

One day that foolish man visited a sage's garden to collect leaves when an angry snake gave him a fatal bite. Susharma's death led him to many hells where he suffered a long time for his sins. Eventually he took birth as a bull and was bought by a crippled man who used him as a beast of burden. For seven or eight years that bull worked extremely hard until one day he collapsed unconscious on the ground, exhausted from the load he was made to carry.

In pity, many kind-hearted people gathered around and offered the bull their blessings.

In the crowd

that gathered, there was also a prostitute who gave to that bull the results of her good works even though she was unsure if she had ever performed any. The bull then died.

The Lord of Death, Yamaraja, informed him "You are now free from all your sins because of the blessings of a certain prostitute." Susharma was then born into a high-class *brahmana* family and was able to remember his previous lives. Driven by burning curiosity, that blessed *brahmana* searched out the prostitute. He introduced himself, told his story and asked her "My dear lady, what action did you perform to enable me to become free from my sins? Please explain this to me?"

The prostitute replied, "Dear Sir, I keep a parrot in a cage and everyday I hear that bird recite a certain hymn that has a wonderfully purifying effect on my heart. I believe that the result of hearing that hymn was that I acquired some *punya*, or piety, and I was able, through my blessing, to pass this on to you. Let us inquire from the bird himself, so that we may find out the truth."

Upon being asked, the parrot, who also remembered his previous life, began to tell his story. He said, "In the past I was a proud and jealous *brahmana* and due to my offensive nature I would insult other learned persons. Because of this, when I died, I was cast down to hell and suffered horribly for a long time. Eventually I acquired this parrot's body that you now see. However, this is not all. Because of my past sins, my mother and father died when I was not long out of the egg. By good fortune some *rishis* saw me lying unprotected on the hot sands and rescued me. They took me to their hermitage and kept me in a cage. More good fortune ensured that those *rishis* regularly taught their children the first chapter of *Bhagavad-gita*. Hearing them repeat those verses, I was also able to learn them. Soon after I was stolen by a thief and sold to this good lady."

Inspired and amazed by this story, Susharma also learned the words of the first chapter of *Bhagavad-gita* then went on his way. Soon after, he became an enlightened soul.

Lord Vishnu concluded, "By the regular recitation of the first chapter of *Bhagavad-gita*, the parrot, the prostitute and Susharma all became completely pure and rose up to the spiritual world, Vaikuntha."

Lord Shiva then explained to Goddess Parvati, "Anyone who hears, studies or recites the first chapter of *Bhagavad-gita* easily pass over the ocean of birth and death and engage in the divine service of Lord Krishna."

The Brahmana, Tiger, Goat and Monkey

Lord Shiva said: "My dear Parvati, as you have enjoyed hearing the glories of the first chapter of *Bhagavad-gita* I shall continue with the second." There is a town in the South of India called Pandharpur where a wise *brahmana* called Devashyama lived. There were few *brahmanas* who could equal him in the performance of fire sacrifices. Additionally, he took great care in receiving guests and so earned the favour of the gods. In spite of all this he was not satisfied at heart because he felt that his knowledge was incomplete.

Devashyama desired to develop his relationship with Lord Krishna, He who resides in the hearts of all living beings, and for that purpose Devashyama

served many *yogis* and holy men hoping for guidance in this matter. Finally after many years he was fortunate enough to meet such a person, one who could guide him onto the right path. It happened in the following way.

One day, Devashyama saw a *yogi* sitting cross-legged and fixed in a trance. On witnessing his completely peaceful condition, Devashyama humbly approached that *yogi* and fell at his feet begging for guidance.

The *yogi*, smiling kindly, directed Devashyama to the village of Sowpur where he was to contact a God-realised goat-herder called Mitravan and take guidance from him. Devashyama was extremely grateful and repeatedly offered his respects to the *yogi's* feet. He then left.

Upon arriving in Sowpur he discovered a beautiful forest on the northern

side. It was there that he found Mitravan sitting on some rocks by a river. It was a beautiful scene with soft breezes wafting the fragrance of wild flowers in all directions while the river's waters rippled by making continuous and delightful sounds that served as background music to the cooing of doves. Amidst all of this, Mitravan's goats were wandering here and there completely undisturbed by the presence of ferocious beasts like tigers.

Beholding this wonderful scene, Devashyama's mind became totally peaceful and in this state he humbly approached Mitravan and introduced himself. Mitravan patiently heard Devashyama's questions in regard to attaining devotion to Lord Krishna and after careful thought he gave this reply:

20

"Many moons ago, while herding my goats in the forest, a hungry tiger attacked us. Out of fear we scattered in all directions. From a safe distance I looked back and saw that the tiger had cornered one of the goats and was about to devour him. At at that moment something very strange and wonderful happened. The mood of the tiger suddenly changed from ferocious anger to peaceful serenity. He relaxed his grip on the goat who was quite astonished by the change."

"The goat said, "Dear tiger, are you playing some cruel game? I don't understand why you are not devouring my flesh with great satisfaction."

"To this the tiger replied, "I myself do not understand. I am overcome by a great sense of peace and satisfaction. It seems that all hunger and thirst has left me and gone to a distant place."

"Noticing a monkey sitting on a branch in a nearby tree the tiger prompted, "Dear goat, let us approach this monkey. He looks as though he knows something." They both approached the monkey and asked for an explanation. The monkey softly laughed and with great respect informed them of a very ancient story."

"Deep in this forest there is a magnificent temple in which Lord Brahma placed a *Shivalinga* (sacred stone) to be worshipped. The *Shivalinga* was worshipped everyday by a sage who offered it fresh forest flowers and clean river water. That sage was Sukarma and he continued this service for many years."

"One day a holy man visited the temple and as a good host Sukarma fed him nice fruits and water. Being pleased by the service of Sukarma that holy man taught him knowledge of Lord Krishna and inscribed on a stone slab the second chapter of the *Bhagavad-gita*. He then left, but not before instructing Sukarma to daily recite the words of those verses with great devotion. Sukarma practiced this for the rest of his life and by doing so gained the full mercy of

Lord Krishna, which saved him from hunger, thirst and anxiety."

"Because of those wonderful activities which were performed here, and because of the presence of the verses on the stone, anyone who visits this place immediately gets full relief from the pangs of hunger and thirst and all types of distress," Thus concluded the monkey.

Mitravan continued, "Dear Devashyama, after hearing that wonderful story, I went with the goat and tiger to visit that temple which housed the inscribed stone and I read over and over again those wonderful verses of chapter two of *Bhagavad-gita*. In this way we attained devotion to Lord Krishna. You also, my friend, can achieve the same success simply by faithfully reciting the second chapter of *Bhagavad-gita*."

Lord Shiva concluded, "And so, My dear Queen, Devashyama was divinely blessed by the instruction of Mitravan and returned home to Pandharpur where he continued to daily recite the second chapter. He would also recite it to anyone willing to listen."

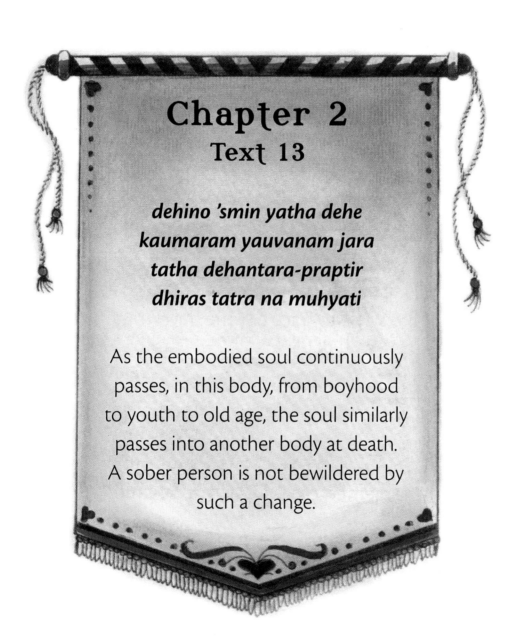

Chapter 2
Text 13

dehino 'smin yatha dehe
kaumaram yauvanam jara
tatha dehantara-praptir
dhiras tatra na muhyati

As the embodied soul continuously passes, in this body, from boyhood to youth to old age, the soul similarly passes into another body at death. A sober person is not bewildered by such a change.

The Ghost attains a Vishnu Form

Jada the *brahmana* lived in a town called Janasthan. He was born in the dynasty of Kaushik. Jada abandoned the religious duties that are prescribed in the scriptures and instead took to a life of hunting, gambling, drinking and other vices.

After wasting his money in this way, he decided to take a business trip to the northern countries, which he promptly did. After gaining much wealth he began his journey back home. Some days later, having covered a long distance, he found himself in a very deserted place. As darkness slowly descended he settled down to take rest under a tree. However, he was discovered by robbers who plundered his wealth and brutally beat him to death. Because Jada had led such a sinful life, the agents of death punished him to become a ghost.

Unlike his father, the son of Jada was a very pious and religious person who had studied all the ancient scriptures and practiced them. Realizing his father's return was long overdue, the son decided to go and search for him. After many days he was able to trace out the travel route his father had taken, and made inquiries to all he met.

Eventually he met a traveller who knew of Jada's death and explained what happened. Upon hearing this, the dutiful son began a journey to Kashi (Benares) to offer *pinda* (worship) for the benefit of his father's soul. By strange co-incidence, at the end of the ninth day of his journey, the son stopped under the same tree where his father had met with the agents of death.

Before taking rest, he performed his daily worship of Lord Krishna and chanted the third chapter of *Bhagavad-gita*. As he completed the recitation, a supernatural sound vibrated in the sky overhead. Looking up he saw an astonishing sight. It was his father, Jada! Before his very eyes, his father's form

changed into that of a divine being resembling Lord Vishnu Himself. He possessed extraordinary features of great beauty and the brightness of his body lit up all directions. Jada showered down blessings and explained to his wonder-struck son the meaning of that event.

"My dear son, because you recited the third chapter of *Bhagavad-gita* I have been released from the ghostly life I received due to past sins. You are a righteous son and I am very pleased with you. As you have now successfully fulfilled your duty, you may return home with my blessings. But there is one thing more before you go. My brother also commited many sins and is suffering the torments of hell. So please release him and any of our ancestors trapped and suffering here and there in many different species of life. As you now know, you can do this by kindly reciting that sweet message of Lord Krishna, the third chapter of *Bhagavad-gita*. By that transcendental activity my ancestors will all receive divine forms, like this one of mine that you now see before you. They will rise up to the spiritual world, never to return again."

Upon hearing this, the selfless son exclaimed "In that case I will continue chanting the third chapter until all the fallen souls in creation are free." Pleased by his noble son's commitment the father said "Let it be so" and entered a glowing aerial chariot, which departed for Vaikuntha (the spiritual world).

The son then returned to Janasthan with a strong desire to liberate all the fallen souls trapped in hell. He meditated upon his deity of Lord Krishna and with great concentration recited the third chapter of the *Bhagavad-gita*.

He continued like this for many days. In this way he gained the attention of Lord Vishnu who was reclining peacefully on the bed of Ananta-Sesha in the ocean of milk.

The Lord called for His messengers, the *Vishnudutas* and instructed them "Go to the kingdom of Yamaraj, the lord of death, with the following message."

"Dear, Yamaraja, my trusted servant, I hope all is well with you. I have something for you to do. Kindly release all the souls suffering in hell. Thank you."

Yamaraja dutifully followed the Lord's instruction and then wisely took the opportunity to personally visit Lord Vishnu. Arriving there at Svetadvip (the ocean of milk) Yamaraj entered the presence of Lord Vishnu. He marvelled at the wondrous scene before him. Lord Vishnu's dazzling form appeared more brilliant than millions of suns as he lay blissfully on the soft white coils of Ananta-Sesha floating in the ocean of milk.

The Goddess of Fortune lovingly massaged the Lord's lotus feet while the chief gods, sages and celestial beings worshipped Him with heart-felt praise and offered continuous prayers. Yamaraja, having had *darshan* (a vision) of the God of gods, offered his humble prostrations and spoke as follows "My Dear Lord, not only do You cause the creation and destruction of these temporary worlds but as the Supersoul You enter into the hearts of all beings and guide them accordingly. You are actually the best well-wishing friend of everyone. You are the guide and the goal. You are timeless and the controller of time. There is no limit to Your glories. Please bless me."

After a pause, Yamaraj continued "Dear Lord, I have followed your instructions and released all those in hell. What now would You have me do?"

Lord Vishnu, smiling mercifully, replied with a voice deep as thunder but as sweet as honey. "Dear God of Justice, I am very pleased with you. Please return to your own abode and continue your service. Even though you have released all of those souls from hell, sadly you will never be without new souls who need to be punished in order to become free from their bad *karma*. Kindly return with my full blessings." That divine vision then disappeared and Yamaraj returned to his duties.

In the meantime Jada's son, who was chanting the third chapter of *Bhagavad-gita*, was taken by the *Vishnudutas* to the abode of Vishnu where he is engaged in the eternal service of the Lord to this very day.

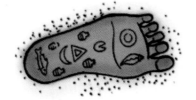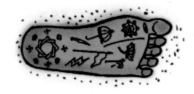

Chapter 3
Text 13

yajna-sistasinah santo
mucyante sarva-kilbisaih
bhunjate te tv agham papa
ye pacanty atma-karanat

The devotees of the Lord are released from all kinds of sins because they eat food which is offered first for sacrifice. Others, who prepare food for personal sense enjoyment, verily eat only sin.

Cursed to Become Trees

Lord Shiva said, "My dear Queen, I will now describe the wonders of the fourth chapter of *Bhagavad-gita*."

There was a great saint called Bharat who lived in a temple on the banks of Mother Ganges at Kashi (Benares). With heart-felt feelings he would daily recite the fourth chapter of *Bhagavad-gita*. He went on pilgrimage to a place called Tapodan where he took *darshan* of Lord Krishna in His Deity form.

Upon leaving that town it became so hot that Bharat sought shade and rest from two *bael* fruit trees. Laying down he used the root of one tree as a foot-rest and the root of the other as a headrest.

After his departure from that place the two trees dried up and died. This happened over the course of five or six days. It so happened that the two souls that inhabited those trees went on to take birth as the daughters of a righteous *brahmana*. When the girls reached seven years of age that *brahmana* arranged for them to go on pilgrimage to Kashi (Benares). As they were visiting that holy place those fortunate girls met the great sage Bharat.

Upon seeing him they had a vivid remembrance of their former lives and fell at his feet. "O Maharaj Bharat, you delivered us. It was by your mercy we are now freed from those tree forms."

The sober sage opened his eyes wide in surprise and eagerly inquired from them, "Dear daughters, I know nothing of what you say. Please explain everything to me?"

The girls, who could recall their former lives, began to explain. One girl said, "Maharaj, there was a great *rishi* who performed many difficult disciplines. He lived at a holy place called Chinnapaap on the banks of the Godavari River. In the heat of the summer he would sit surrounded by many fires and in the winter he would stand in the chilling waters of the river. In this way he developed complete control over his senses and achieved the favour of the Supreme Lord, Krishna. This *rishi* became so pure that even Lord Brahma, the most respected of the gods, came to visit him to learn about the truths of Lord Krishna."

"The fame of the *rishi's* power grew and grew until it reached the ears of Lord Indra, the king of heaven. Indra however, considered the *rishi's* greatness to be a threat and became scared that he would take over his position as king of heaven. Desiring to protect his throne, Indra called for us to help him and

so we took birth as heavenly dancing girls and Indra commanded "Go to where the *rishi* is performing his strict meditation and distract him with your dancing. He will then lose his power." Following his instructions we went to the bank of the Godavari River and sang very romantic songs as we slowly moved before him with our perfumed bodies. We tried to tease him with our dancing and the sound of our ankle bells but that powerful *rishi* was not to be tempted. Instead he expressed great anger, touched water and cursed us to stand naked as *bael* trees on the banks of the Ganga. We were immediately grief-stricken and fell at the rishi's feet begging forgiveness."

"We explained that we were simply carrying out the instructions of Lord Indra. That sage was merciful and forgave us, but the curse could not be taken back. So he blessed us that we could remember all our previous lives and would be released from the tree forms when Maharaj Bharat came to us. So cast your mind back, Maharaj, to when you visited and rested beneath two *bael* trees. We were those trees at that time. You chanted the *shlokas* (verses) of the fourth chapter of *Bhagavad-gita*. On the strength of that holy recitation and shortly after you left, we were released from the curse and had the good fortune to be born in a family of Krishna devotees. Not only that but we lost all interest in enjoying this material world."

Lord Shiva concluded "After telling their story to Maharaj Bharat, they all happily left for his *ashram*. The girls continued chanting the fourth chapter of *Bhagavad-gita* and achieved all perfection."

The Vulture and the Parrot

Lord Shiva continued, "Listen very attentively, Oh Parvati, and I will tell you of the glories of the fifth chapter of *Bhagavad-gita*."

Long ago there lived a *brahmana* named Pingala. He resided in the state of Madra. During his childhood he was taught to study the *Vedas* and practise religious duties but actually he had no interest in these things. Upon reaching youth he gave up his pursuits and eagerly involved himself in singing, dancing and playing musical instruments.

With practice he became so skilled a musician and dancer that he attracted the attention of the king. The king invited him to live in the palace, which he did. There were many varieties of enjoyment available in palace life and Pingala soon became very degraded. He regularly became drunk, ate flesh foods and behaved badly with the wives of other men. Becoming a close friend to the king, proud Pingala would criticize others in an unrestricted way. In this manner his sins increased more and more.

Pingala had a wife, Aruna, who in many ways was no better than him. She came from a degraded family and secretly had many secret meetings with other men. One day Pingala discovered Aruna's secret life so she decided to silence him without delay. When he was fast asleep she took a sharp hatchet, chopped off his head and under the cover of darkness buried his body in the garden. Aruna then enjoyed all sorts of sinful activities, became diseased and finally died.

For her sins she suffered in hell for a long time and then took birth as a female parrot. In the meantime, Pingala, after losing his head, also went to hell for a long time and then took birth as a vulture. To find his food, the vulture would circle in the air and scan the ground for movement below while Aruna flew from tree to tree searching for fruits. One

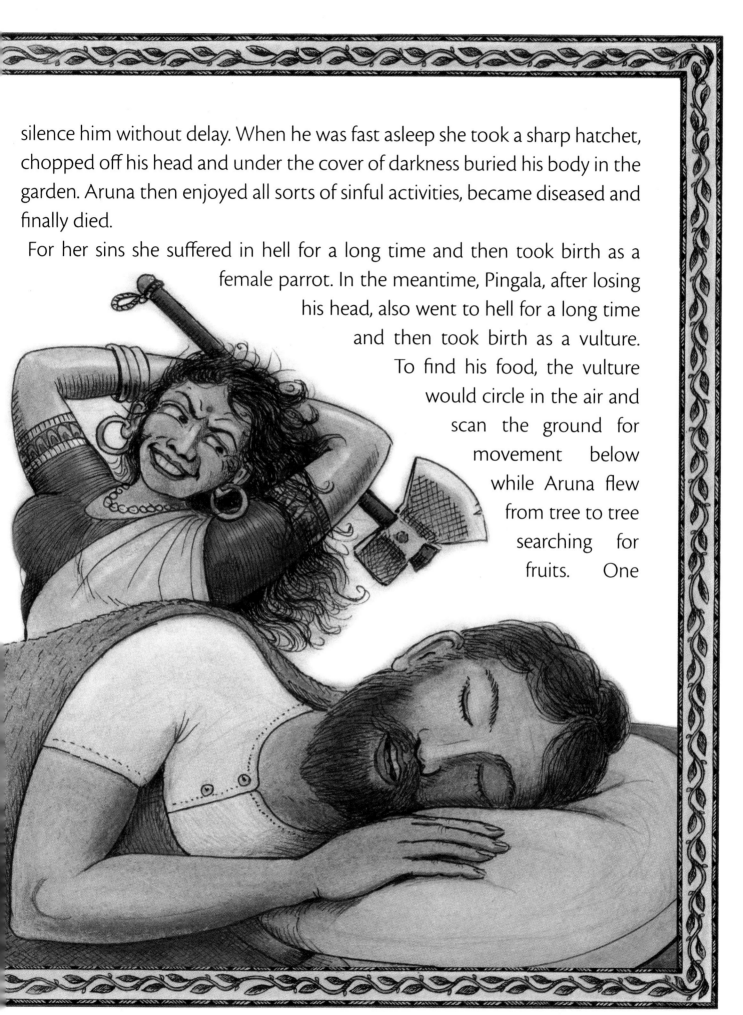

day while looking for food, Pingala the vulture spotted Aruna, the parrot.

At that time Pingala remembered his previous life and swooped down on the female parrot and with great anger ferociously stabbed her with his sharp hooked beak and talons. As she fell dead her head dropped into a human skull.

At that very same moment a hunter who was observing the scene released an arrow from his bow and killed the vulture whose head also fell into the skull.

The lord of death, Yamaraj, sent his messengers, the *Yamadutas*, to bring Pingala and Aruna before him whereupon he informed the couple "You are now freed from all your bad karma and are qualified to enter Vaikuntha." The couple, unable to remember anything good they had done, were surprised at this blessing and begged an explanation.

Yamaraja replied, "There was a pure and exalted devotee called Vat who resided on the banks of the Ganga. He daily recited the fifth chapter of *Bhagavad-gita* and in that way completely perfected his life. Upon leaving his purified body, that devotee boarded a flower aeroplane and went directly to Vaikuntha."

Yamaraja continued, "Both of you had the good fortune to contact the skull of Vat's body and by the power of his devotion to the fifth chapter of *Bhagavad-gita* you too have become fit to enter Vaikuntha."

Lord Shiva concluded, "My dear Parvati, after hearing the explanation of Yamaraja both Pingala and Aruna became very happy and boarded a sky-chariot, which had come to take them to the spiritual realm. Such are the glories of the fifth chapter of *Bhagavad-gita*."

The Great Sage Raikva

Long, long ago in a town called Paithan, on the bank of the Godavari river, ruled a famous king by the name of Janshruti. That king was devoted to the gods and to the welfare of his people. Every day he performed costly fire sacrifices that were so large and magnificent, the smoke from them spiralled right up to the heavens above.

King Janshruti created lakes, had wells dug and generously gave all types of gifts to the citizens, just as a great rain-cloud distributes life-giving water upon fertile land.

Due to his constant acts of sacrifice, crops flourished, rain fell only at night and unwanted rodents like rats simply disappeared. Because of Janshruti's pure religious activities, the citizens felt themselves truly blessed to have such a king.

The gods were also pleased with King Janshruti so they decided to visit him. Taking the forms of white swans they flew together over his kingdom. Their idea was to personally offer him their blessings. Then something unusual happened.

One swan with two others suddenly broke from the group. In response the other swans called out, "Where are you going dear brothers? Do you not see the great King Janshruti just beneath us on the roof of his palace? He is so powerful that just by his wish alone he can burn up his enemies."

The leader of the break-away swans replied by laughing. "O brothers, I ask you one thing. Is this king as powerful as the great sage Raikva?" The other swans were puzzled by such a reply. But the King below, who

understood the language of birds, witnessed all this and was most pleased. He came down from the high roof of his palace and thought carefully about what he had heard. He decided to call for Maha, his chariot driver.

The king instructed, "Dear Maha, it is my good fortune that I have heard about an exceptionally qualified sage by the name of Raikva. I am not sure where he resides so I want you to find out."

"Search all directions and return only when you find him." Happy to be on such an important mission, Maha bowed to his King and immediately left.

First, he travelled to Kashipuri, then to Gaya. He searched many holy places until he came to Mathura, which is in the shape of a half-moon and is situated on the bank of the sacred River Jamuna. Mathura is the residence of the Supreme Lord, Krishna. All the great demigods, sages and devotees visit or live in Mathura with the purpose of pleasing the Lord in many different ways. Surrounding the area of Mathura are holy *tulasi* bushes, wish-fullfilling trees and twelve wonderful forests where Lord Krishna enjoyed pleasure pastimes with the cows, cowherd boys and cowherd girls. The whole area of Mathura is made even more wonderful by the crowning glory of Goverdhan Hill which Krishna used as an umbrella to protect His devotees from the devastating rains sent by Lord Indra.

After blissfully exploring Mathura, Maha searched for Raikva both in the Western and Northern Provinces. Finally he arrived at the beautiful shining city of Kashmir where all kinds of celebrations were going on to please Lord Shiva who is the presiding Deity there. In that place Lord Shiva is known as Manikeshvara and the King of Kashmir, who had just returned from various places where he defeated many kings in battle, was opulently worshipping him. The king was so devoted to Lord Shiva that he was also known by the name Manikeshvara. Many sacrificial fires burned brightly in that fair city and because of this the smoke from them formed rows of clouds which hung over the city like a festive decoration. The atmosphere was such that even the common people appeared as beautiful as demigods.

Maha took great pleasure in witnessing all this and just as he was passing the entrance of an exquisite temple, his eyes fell upon the uncommon features of the great sage Raikva. He was beneath a tree sitting on a small cart. Beholding his radiant form, Maha immediately felt within his heart that this must be the great soul he was searching for.

Falling at Raikva's feet, Maha begged him "Oh, great sage, please tell me your name and place of residence. I can see you are a great personality. Please tell me of your purpose here?"

Raikva was unmoved by the enthusiastic words of Maha and contemplated the situation for some moments. He then replied in a grave voice "I am known as Raikva. I am completely satisfied and require nothing."

Maha's heart was thrilled to hear such elevated words. He knew his king would be pleased with the success of his mission so he immediately left that place and sped homeward without delay.

After the long journey back to Paithan, Maha humbled himself before King Janshruti and told him everything.

"Well done," the king exclaimed, "Prepare my swiftest chariot and fill it with precious gifts. Tomorrow at sunrise we depart."

The following morning they left at full speed for Kashmir and after a considerable time, finally arrived there. Having entered the city, Maha immediately took the king to the place where the sage Raikva was staying. Delighted to see the famous sage, the king fell at his feet and offered him gifts of fine silks and rare jewels.

The great sage, however, became most angry and said "You fool, what need do I have for these useless things. Take them away this instant and go."

The King, understanding his mistake, fell again at the feet of the sage and

begged his forgiveness. He pleaded, "I am just a materialistic fool with no knowledge of the self but you have perfected a high state of detachment and devotion to God. Therefore please give me instruction so I too may be saved."

Raikva was satisfied with the king's humble submission. With a smile on his face, he gently explained "I daily recite the beautiful verses of the sixth chapter of *Bhagavad-gita* spoken by Lord Krishna Himself. Stay and I will teach you those same verses by which your life will become completely perfect."

From that day on King Janshruti faithfully recited those verses and in due course of time a celestial airplane descended and took him to Vaikuntha. Shortly after, the great sage Raikva was also transported to Vaikuntha where he continued in the eternal service of the lotus feet of the Supreme Personality of Godhead, Lord Krishna.

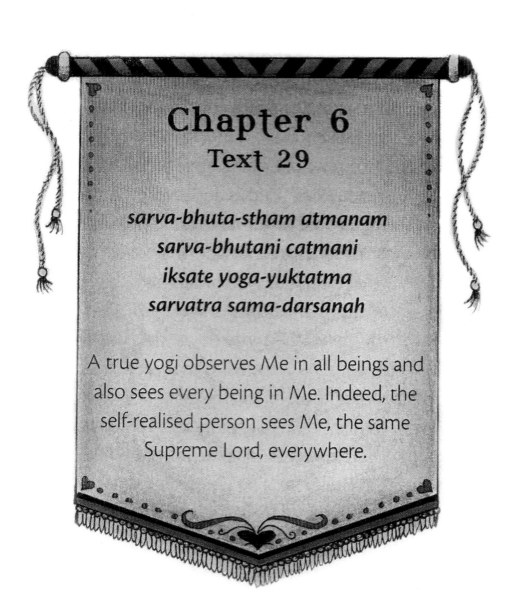

Chapter 6
Text 29

sarva-bhuta-stham atmanam
sarva-bhutani catmani
iksate yoga-yuktatma
sarvatra sama-darsanah

A true yogi observes Me in all beings and also sees every being in Me. Indeed, the self-realised person sees Me, the same Supreme Lord, everywhere.

The Treasure
of the
Snake Ghost

Lord Shiva said "My dear Parvati, hear now the divine glories of the seventh chapter of *Bhagavad-gita*."

Shankukarna was a so-called *brahmana* who lived in a large town called Pataliputra. Like an atheist, he performed no devotional service to Lord Krishna, and neglected the religious ceremonies that would release his departed forefathers from whatever sinful conditions of life they may have been in.

Shankukarna's main concern was to amass huge amounts of wealth by the performance of business activities. In this endeavour he was so successful that even great kings would come as guests to his luxurious house and dine there. In spite of his vast fortune, greed made Shankukarna into the worst of misers — so much so that he uselessly hoarded his riches deep under the ground in a secret place, the whereabouts of which only he knew.

Even in his family life, Shankukarna was never satisfied, for although he had children from three wives, he planned to marry yet again. He travelled with his relatives to another town to marry his fourth wife, and stopped overnight on the way. While he was sleeping, a venomous snake gave him a fatal bite. His sons and relatives tried to revive him with medicines and *mantras* but everything failed.

In his next life Shankukarna became a *preta-sarp*, a snake-ghost, and because he could remember his last life, he went directly to the place where his wealth was hoarded.

This, of course, was quite close to where his previous family were living. He was content for some time to simply guard his hoard but soon became frustrated with his life as a *preta-sarp*, so he appeared in the dreams of his sons and asked them for help. He said to each of them "I am your dead father and I am now living as a *preta-sarp* guarding a great amount of treasure that I want to share between you." He then told them where it was.

In the morning the sons woke and told each other of their dreams. One son, Shiva, suspected these were more than just dreams which coincided with each other. Shiva, like his father, was also greedy for money, so he took a spade and hastily went to the place described in the dream and started digging even though a large snake-hole was there. The *preta-sarp* happened to be sleeping at that time and awoke, startled.

The *preta-sarp* came out of the ground hissing loudly and began to sway back and forth in a threatening way. "How dare you disturb me, you fool! Who are you and what is your purpose? Who sent you? Answer me now."

Shiva, understanding the situation immediately replied "I am your son, Shiva. Last night you came to me in a dream and told me come for the treasure."

The *preta-sarp* was pleased with the reply and laughed. "Yes, but you have forgotten something. If you are truly my son, why are you not performing the necessary rituals to free me from this snake form? It is due to greed only that I am cursed like this. Do you want to meet the same fate as myself?"

Responding to this challenge the ignorant son humbly asked his father "What exactly should I do?"

"My dear son" replied the *preta-sarp*, "No type of charity, penance or sacrifice will bring me complete happiness or total freedom. Only by the recitation of the seventh chapter of *Bhagavad-gita* can I be saved from the wheel of birth and death. Therefore kindly seek out a pure *brahmana* who knows this chapter, and at the time of performing the *shraddha* ceremony, feed him

very nicely. The *shraddha* rituals can remove my sins, but the seventh chapter of *Bhagavad-gita* can open the door of Vaikuntha. Therefore kindly do this for me."

Desiring to please their father, Shiva and his brothers performed the *shraddha* rituals while a qualified *brahmana* chanted the seventh chapter of *Bhagavad-gita*. By the power of those verses, Shankukarna became free from the snake-ghost body and received a spiritual four-armed form (*sarupya mukti*). He then blessed his sons and ascended to the spiritual world.

The blessed sons developed devotion to Lord Krishna by using their wealth to construct temples, distribute food and dig wells. They daily recited the seventh chapter of *Bhagavad-gita* and finally attained the same destination as their father.

Lord Shiva concluded "My dear Parvati, anyone who hears this narration will certainly be freed from all sinful reactions."

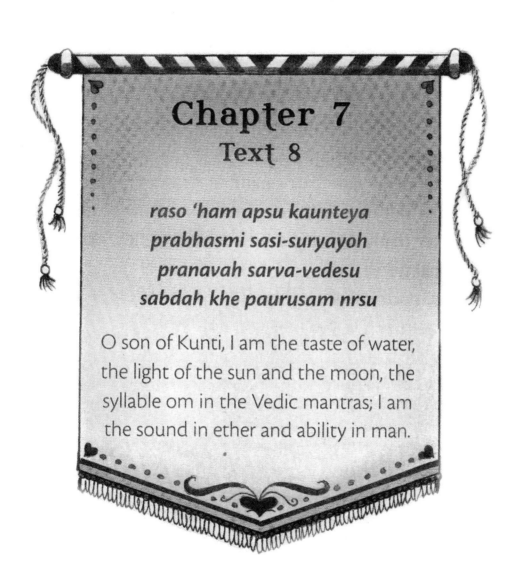

Chapter 7
Text 8

raso 'ham apsu kaunteya
prabhasmi sasi-suryayoh
pranavah sarva-vedesu
sabdah khe paurusam nrsu

O son of Kunti, I am the taste of water, the light of the sun and the moon, the syllable om in the Vedic mantras; I am the sound in ether and ability in man.

Two Ghosts
and a
Date Palm Tree

Lord Shiva said "My dear Parvati, the divine power of the *Bhagavad-gita* is unlimited. Please listen now and I will describe the glories of the eighth chapter. It will bring joy to your heart."

There was once a fallen *brahmana* by the name of Bhavasharma. He lived in the South of India in a town called Amardhakapur. That man got married but spent most of his time stealing, hunting, eating meat, drinking wine and doing other such sinful things.

Bhavasharma attended many parties and at one such party he drank so much wine that he became very sick. That sinful man developed chronic dysentery and after many days of terrible misery, he left his body. He was reborn as a date palm tree.

After some time, two powerful ghosts (*brahma-rakshasas*) rested under that tree. Listen carefully and I will tell you their history.

Kushibal was a *brahmana* had mastered all the Vedic sciences. In spite of this, he was greedy, and his wife, Kumati, was evil-minded. Daily, they would eagerly collect much charity for themselves, but would share it with no one. As a consequence, when their lives ended, they became *brahma-rakshasas*. In those ghostly forms, they constantly wandered the earth suffering the pangs of hunger and thirst until one fateful day they decided to take rest under that date palm tree.

Tired of their miserable existence, the wife begged her husband "How can we ever get free of this wretched life? I can endure it no more!"

Remembering his former studies, the husband replied "Only by knowledge of *Brahman* (universal spirit), the self and proper actions do we have hope of freeing ourselves from this cursed condition."

The wife then asked *"Kim tad brahma kim adhyatmam kim karma purusottama"* which means, O my Lord, what is *Brahman*? What is the self? And what are proper actions? Without realizing it the wife had repeated word for word half of the first verse of the eighth chapter of the *Bhagavad-gita*. Then something wonderful happened. To their utter amazement, the date palm tree vanished and in its place stood a *brahmana*. What had happened was that by the extraordinary power of those words, Bhavasharma was immediately released from the form of the date palm tree and again became a *brahmana*, freed from all sins.

Suddenly there appeared in the sky a beautiful flower-airplane. When it landed, the husband and wife were released from their *brahma-rakshasa* forms, and to their astonishment attained divine bodies with which they alighted the waiting aircraft and ascended to the Vaikuntha regions.

Amazed after witnessing all of this, Bhavasharma the *brahmana* was so moved that he dutifully committed to writing those divine words – *Kim tad brahma kim adhyatmam kim dharma purushottama*. He then travelled to Kashipuri, on the banks of the river Ganges, and as a means of pleasing the Supreme Lord he continuously chanted that half-*shloka*, while performing great austerities.

Lord Vishnu was most pleased by the unswerving determination of Bhavasharma, and not only awarded him entrance to the spiritual world, but gave the same blessings to all his ancestors also.

Lord Shiva concluded "Dear Parvati, thus I have described to you just a glimpse into the glories of the eighth chapter of *Bhagavad-gita*."

Chapter 8
Text 16

a brahma-bhuvanal lokah
punar avartino 'rjuna
mam upetya tu kaunteya
punar janma na vidyate

From the highest planet in the material world down to the lowest, all are places of misery wherein repeated birth and death take place. But one who attains to My abode, O son of Kunti, never takes birth again.

The Goat Sacrifice

Lord Shiva continued, "My dear Parvati, please hear the glories of the ninth chapter of *Bhagavad-gita*."

Madhava, a very strict *brahmana*, lived in Mahismati, a town situated on the banks of the Narmada River. He was very learned, and was so skilled in the performance of religious sacrifices, that he received many gifts of charity from his rich supporters. With his great wealth he decided to perform a costly fire sacrifice that began with the ritual sacrifice of a goat. Madhava instructed his assistants to first clean the animal very nicely before offering it into the fire.

To everybody's great surprise, the goat laughed very loudly, just like a human being, and then spoke the following words to Madhava, who was conducting the sacrifice "You fool! You are supposed to be learned, but what is the actual benefit of performing sacrifices that simply bind you to the continuous cycle of birth and death?"

The gathering of people was astonished to hear these words from the goat. Madhava humbly submitted this reply. "I am simply amazed at what you said. Please tell us of your previous life? What was your occupation? What did you do to become a goat?"

The goat replied "Like you, I was born in a very pious family and dutifully performed all the Vedic rituals recommended for a good life. However, my son became seriously ill and for his recovery my wife urged me to offer a sacrificial goat at the temple of Mother Durga."

As we were offering the life of that goat, the animal cursed me "Cruel and sinful wretch, for this wicked act your children will be fatherless. Therefore, I curse you to become a goat like me. And that, O Madhava, is how I became

a goat." The *brahmana* was wonderstruck to hear this story from the mouth of the goat. "If you think that is amazing" continued the goat "Here is another story. Listen if you will."

"In the holy land known as Kurukshetra, there lived the great King Chandrasharma. He appeared in the dynasty of Suryadev, the sun-god. At the auspicious time of the solar eclipse, the king desired to give all types of charity to a qualified *brahmana*. First he bathed in a sacred lake. Then he dressed in clean white cloth and smeared some sandalwood paste on his body. Accompanied by a priest, he then approached a respectable *brahmana*. Among the many gifts he offered was a servant, whose body was completely black, and as that servant approached the *brahmana* something most strange happened. The servant's chest heaved and out came the mystical forms of a dog-eater and his wife. These forms immediately entered the body of the *brahmana*. In this way two *chandalas* were transferred from one body to another. The *brahmana*, with complete control over his mind and senses meditated on the lotus feet of Lord Govinda and calmly chanted the ninth chapter of the *Bhagavad-gita*."

"Almost immediately the order-carriers of Vishnu, the *Vishnudutas*, arrived on the scene and dragged those two sinful dog-eaters out of the body of the *brahmana* and drove them to a distant place. The *brahmana*, unmoved, continued chanting."

"In the meantime, the King, who was witnessing all this, simply stood there rooted to the spot and then eagerly inquired "O *brahmana*, who were those two persons? What *mantras* are you chanting? What is your meditation? Please tell me for I have never seen anything so extraordinary before."

"The *brahmana* replied, "O King, the *chandala* was the personality of sin and his wicked wife was the personality of offensiveness. For protection I chanted the divine words of the ninth chapter of *Bhagavad-gita*. Those divine words, that originally issued forth from the sacred mouth of Lord Govinda, grant one all protection in the face of the greatest danger. I simply meditate on His divine feet and remember those verses and in this way become fearless."

"Upon receiving this information the King was so inspired that he too learned the verses of the ninth chapter of *Bhagavad-gita* and by remembering the feet of Lord Govinda, made his life perfect." Thus the goat concluded his speech.

Madhava, deciding to follow the good example of the King, also learned the ninth chapter of *Bhagavad-gita* and made his life perfect also.

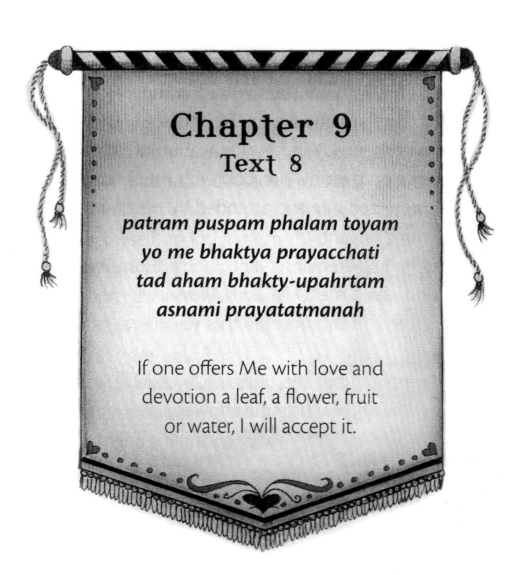

Chapter 9
Text 8

patram puspam phalam toyam
yo me bhaktya prayacchati
tad aham bhakty-upahrtam
asnami prayatatmanah

If one offers Me with love and devotion a leaf, a flower, fruit or water, I will accept it.

The Great Black Swan

Lord Shiva said "Dear Parvati, Please hear carefully the glories of the tenth chapter of the *Bhagavad-gita* and you will surely be filled with wonder."

"As you well know, I am constantly fixed in thinking of Lord Krishna, and others who do the same are my life and soul. One such devotee, Dhirabuddhi, was so steady in his glorification of Lord Krishna, that I was completely won over by him, and with much love I followed his movements, protected him and attended his needs whenever I could, just like a humble servant."

Seeing all this, my eternal servant Bhringiriddhi, was overcome by curiosity and asked me "Dear Lord, Please tell me the history and special qualities of this devotee that you are taking such pleasure in serving?"

"Responding to the question, I replied, "Some time ago in Kailash, I was sitting in a flower garden during the evening. The moon was shining brightly and it was

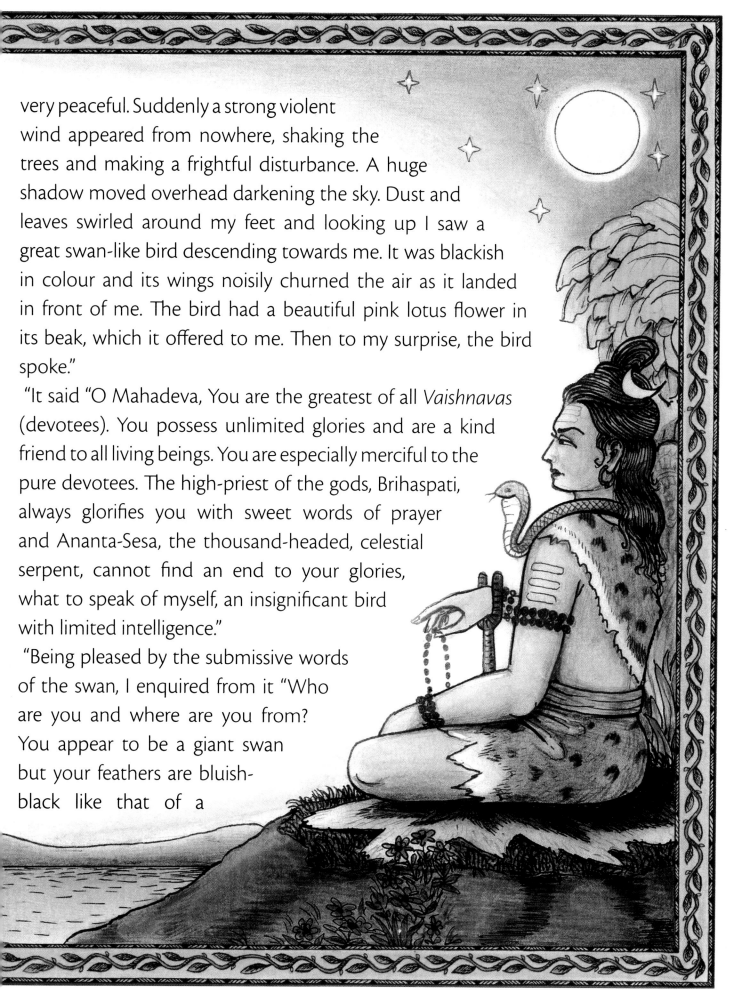

very peaceful. Suddenly a strong violent wind appeared from nowhere, shaking the trees and making a frightful disturbance. A huge shadow moved overhead darkening the sky. Dust and leaves swirled around my feet and looking up I saw a great swan-like bird descending towards me. It was blackish in colour and its wings noisily churned the air as it landed in front of me. The bird had a beautiful pink lotus flower in its beak, which it offered to me. Then to my surprise, the bird spoke."

"It said "O Mahadeva, You are the greatest of all *Vaishnavas* (devotees). You possess unlimited glories and are a kind friend to all living beings. You are especially merciful to the pure devotees. The high-priest of the gods, Brihaspati, always glorifies you with sweet words of prayer and Ananta-Sesa, the thousand-headed, celestial serpent, cannot find an end to your glories, what to speak of myself, an insignificant bird with limited intelligence."

"Being pleased by the submissive words of the swan, I enquired from it "Who are you and where are you from? You appear to be a giant swan but your feathers are bluish-black like that of a crow. Please explain everything to me."

"The swan replied "Thank you Mahadev. I am actually the carrier of Lord Brahma and I will now tell you how I became this blackish colour."

"The heavenly lotus flower that I just offered to you came from a beautiful lake near Surat. One day while flying over that lake my wings became paralysed and I fell down into the water. I then discovered, much to my surprise, that my snow-white body had turned as black as dark clouds."

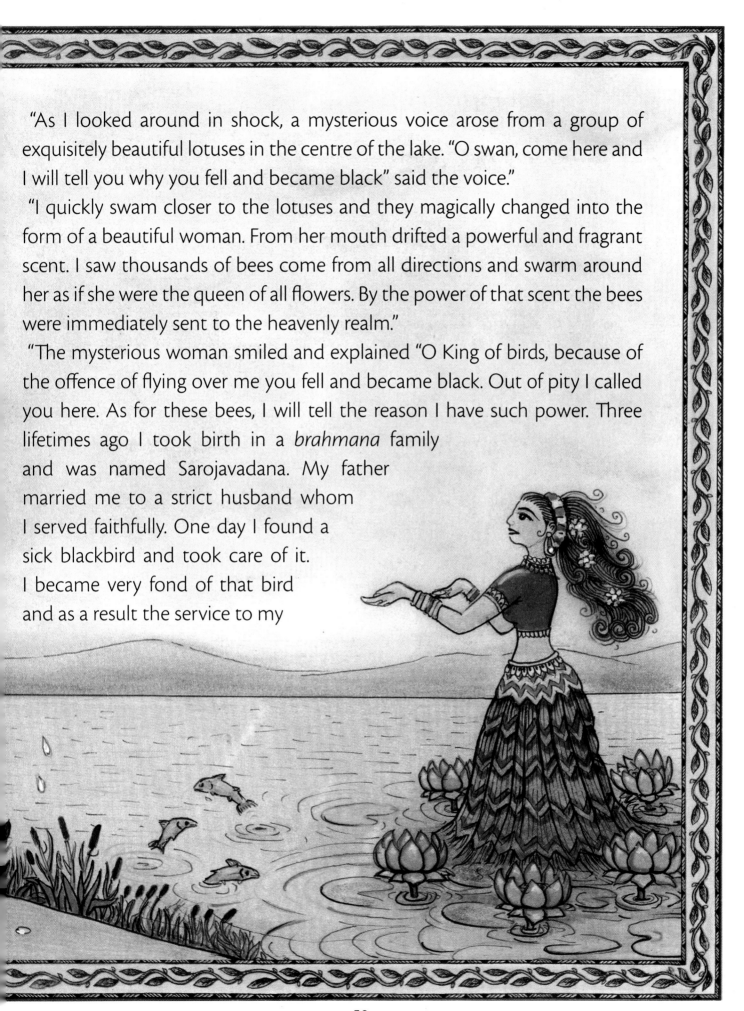

"As I looked around in shock, a mysterious voice arose from a group of exquisitely beautiful lotuses in the centre of the lake. "O swan, come here and I will tell you why you fell and became black" said the voice."

"I quickly swam closer to the lotuses and they magically changed into the form of a beautiful woman. From her mouth drifted a powerful and fragrant scent. I saw thousands of bees come from all directions and swarm around her as if she were the queen of all flowers. By the power of that scent the bees were immediately sent to the heavenly realm."

"The mysterious woman smiled and explained "O King of birds, because of the offence of flying over me you fell and became black. Out of pity I called you here. As for these bees, I will tell the reason I have such power. Three lifetimes ago I took birth in a *brahmana* family and was named Sarojavadana. My father married me to a strict husband whom I served faithfully. One day I found a sick blackbird and took care of it. I became very fond of that bird and as a result the service to my husband suffered. He became most frustrated and in a fit of anger cursed me to become a blackbird in my next life. This happened, and due to some good *karma* I was taken care of by some holy men who kept me at their *ashram*. Twice a day they would chant the tenth chapter of *Bhagavad-gita* and I would listen attentively."

"This resulted in me being elevated to the heavenly planets in my following life where I assumed the form of an *apsara* by the name of Padmavati. I enjoyed life there and often travelled in my flower-aeroplane."

"One day I flew over an enchanting lake filled with fragrant lotus flowers. I descended, desiring to refresh myself in the clear inviting waters. Casting off my clothes I entered those waters and splashed about in great happiness. But, as chance would have it, the short-tempered sage Durvasa Muni happened to pass by and saw me naked. Out of fear I immediately turned myself into five lotuses. My legs and arms became four lotuses and my body and head became the fifth. That fiery sage could not tolerate what he saw, so angrily he cursed me "You sinful creature. May you remain as you are for one hundred autumns." He then continued on his way.

Fortunately, I was able to remember my previous life as a blackbird, and also the words of the tenth chapter of *Bhagavad-gita*. This gave me strength over the passing years. Today the curse has ended, and by coincidence you flew over me, but I am sure that if you learn the tenth chapter of *Bhagavad-gita* from me then you will be freed from this embarrassing situation. Please do this."

"I readily agreed and she taught me those divine verses originally spoken by Lord Krishna. Then a sky chariot came and took Padmavati to Vaikuntha. I have just come from there now to offer you a flower from that lake."

Lord Shiva concluded "Having taken my *darshan*, the black swan gave up his body and took birth in a *brahmana* family as Dhirabuddhi, who with a pure heart always chants the tenth chapter of *Bhagavad-gita*. His chanting is so powerful that whoever hears it, whether they are drunkards or murderers, will certainly be blessed by the *darshan* of Lord Krishna. The same can be said for whoever chants the tenth chapter; they will certainly obtain the same result, regardless of who they are."

A Curse and a Blessing

Lord Shiva continued, "My dear Parvati, I will now tell you a wonderful story in connection with the eleventh chapter of *Bhagavad-gita*. There are numerous stories that glorify this chapter but this one is especially pleasing to hear. Listen and I will tell you."

There was once a pure *brahmana* named Sunanda, who lived in a large town called Megankara, on the banks of the river Pranita. In that town was a temple in which the famous deity of Jagat Isvara resided, bow in hand. Sunanda the *brahmana* daily visited that temple. Sitting before the deity, he meditated on the universal form of the Lord whilst chanting the eleventh chapter of the *Bhagavad-gita*. In this way he became completely satisfied in remembrance of the Lord. One day Sunanda and his friends decided to visit all the holy places on the banks of the Godavari. At each place they bathed and took *darshan* of the local deity. Everything was going well until they reached the town of Vivaha-Tirtha. Arriving there in the late afternoon they searched for a place to stay and eventually found a guesthouse in which they settled for the night. When the sun rose in the morning, Sunanda woke up, and much to his surprise, discovered his companions were missing. After searching around for some time he met the head man of the town and asked for an explanation. The head man immediately fell at the feet of Sunanda and said "O great soul, I am unable to give you a proper explanation, but I can tell you there is no devotee greater than you. Please bless this town with your presence for a few days. I beg this favour of you."

Sunanda, being a kind-hearted *brahmana* agreed to the head man's humble request and hoped also to discover what had happened to his friends. The head man promptly arranged a very comfortable place for him to stay and provided servants and cooks to serve him both day and night.

Time flew by peacefully, but on the eighth day, Sunanda was approached by a weeping villager, who ran up to him and lamented "O pure *brahmana*, last night a wicked man-eating *rakshasa* devoured my son, please help me, please help me." Sunanda placed a comforting arm around the man's shoulder and replied "Dear friend, tell me what happened. Explain everything to me."

The villager continued, "In this town lives a huge, frightful *rakshasa* who feeds on human flesh. He used to snatch us as he pleased, until we made an agreement with him. He agreed to protect us if we provided his food. So we quickly constructed a guest-house with the intention that all travellers who came to the town would be directed to that place. While sleeping, that *rakshasa* would eat them." "Then something wonderful happened," continued the villager, "When your party stayed at that place, all were eaten except you and I shall explain why. Last night I sent a young visitor to stay at the inn, not realising he was a close friend of my son. When my son discovered what had happened, he immediately ran there, hoping to save his friend. Fearing the worst when my son failed to return home, I hurried to the inn and confronted the *rakshasa*." "Did you eat the two boys?" I demanded.

"Yes, they were delicious" he replied with a hideous, broad grin on his face.

"But one was my son" I lamented.

"How was I to know? It was dark." he replied.

Out of desperation, I begged him. "Is there any way he can be restored to life?" The *rakshasa* replied "I am glad you have asked me this question; I think all of this is indeed the will of the Lord. Listen carefully to what I have to say. Last week there was a pure-hearted *brahmana* staying at the guesthouse. I quickly killed and devoured his friends, but spared him because he was chanting the eleventh chapter of *Bhagavad-gita*. I know for certain that if that *brahmana* recites the eleventh chapter seven times and sprinkles water on my head I shall surely be freed from the curse of this *rakshasa* body and your son will be restored to life."

"My heart swelled up with great hope and so I hurried here to see you, but before leaving that *rakshasa*, I was overcome with burning curiosity and asked him to tell me about his curse. His story was as follows."

A long time ago there was a farmer living not far from here. To protect his crops from wild animals he would often stay up all night to guard the fields. One morning a traveller passed by the field close to where the farmer was sitting. Just then a large hungry vulture descended from the sky and started to claw and jab at the defenceless traveller, who cried out for help. A *yogi*, who was on the road at some distance, ran quickly to defend the traveller, but he was too late.

Inflamed with anger, the *yogi* strode over to the farmer and cursed him in the following way, "One who can help others who are

65

endangered by fire, snakes, thieves or weapons but fails to do so is punished by Yamaraj, the god of death. Certainly he will go to hell for a long time and then take birth as a wolf. On the other hand, one who helps those in need pleases Lord Vishnu for sure. Anyone who protects a cow from a wild animal, a cruel man or a wicked king will achieve Lord Vishnu without a doubt. As for you, wicked farmer, you made no attempt to save that traveller from the savage vulture that is devouring his flesh even as I now speak. Therefore I curse you to take birth as a flesh-eating *rakshasa*, because that is what you deserve."

The unfortunate farmer pleaded with the *yogi*, "Please be merciful to me, gentle sage, I have been awake all night, guarding the fields, and was simply too exhausted to rescue the traveller, otherwise I certainly would have done so."

The *yogi* softened, feeling sorry for the farmer, and granted him the following benediction. "You will become free from this curse when a person who daily recites the eleventh chapter of *Bhagavad-gita* sprinkles water on your head." That was the *rakshasa's* story.

The villager then continued, "And so, my dear Sunanda, you are in a position to do us a great service. Please help us."

Without another word they both made their way to the residence of the *rakshasa*, who was most pleased to see them. Sunanda started reciting the

eleventh chapter of *Bhagavad-gita* and then sprinkled water over the *rakshasa's* head. Immediately his ugly body changed into a beautiful four-armed form like that of Lord Vishnu. Then all of the many persons the *rakshasa* had eaten appeared, and their forms changed in the same manner. A divine flower-airplane appeared and that glorious assembly moved toward it to be taken to the spiritual world.

"Wait, wait," cried out the villager, "where is my son?"

The person who was previously a *rakshasa* laughed mildly and called one from those assembled there.

"Here is your son" he replied.

Desiring to enlighten his father with spiritual knowledge, the son addressed him in this way: "My dear sir, many times I have been your son, but now by the grace of this pure devotee, Sunanda, I have been mercifully released from the grinding wheel of birth and death, and am now returning to my real home in the spiritual sky. I therefore humbly advise you to serve the lotus feet of Sunanda and learn the eleventh chapter of *Bhagavad-gita* from him. In this way you will also achieve the perfection of life. Of this there is no doubt."

Lord Shiva said "And so, my dear Parvati, the boy rejoined the assembly of liberated souls and departed for Vaikuntha. Thereafter Sunanda taught the boy's father the eleventh chapter of *Bhagavad-gita* and soon after, they also entered the abode of Vaikuntha."

The Prince Saves the King

Lord Shiva said "Dear Parvati, please hear something of the glories of the twelfth chapter of *Bhagavad-gita*. There is an important holy place in the South. It is called Kolbapur and in that town there is a temple wherein resides Maha-Laksmi, the divine queen of Lord Narayana. She is always attended by the *devas* and fulfils all desires."

One day a handsome young prince arrived at Kolbapur. His golden-hued body had broad shoulders and long powerful arms. He first refreshed himself at a lake called Marikanth-tirtha and offered worship to his ancestors. Then he approached and entered the temple of Maha-Laksmi. Falling at her feet he prayed, "O great Goddess, you are the mother of creation and mercifully give shelter to all living beings. Who would not worship you? All glories to you who fulfils all desires, you are the divine energy of Lord Achyuta, the Supreme Lord. O great Protector, you manifest so many wonderful forms such as Ambika, Brahmi, Vannari, Maheshvari, Narasimhi, Indri, Kumari, Chandika, Lakshmi, Savitri and Rohini. All glories to you O merciful One, please bless me."

Maha-Lakshmi was pleased with the prince's humble, heartfelt prayers and responded to him with the following words. "I am most pleased with you, therefore request a boon."

The prince replied "O Mother of Creation, I am the son of the late King Brahadratha who died before completing the *Ashwamedha* sacrifice. As his son, I desire to complete this sacrifice on his behalf, but the ceremonial horse has been stolen. I have sent persons far and wide and in all directions to find the horse, but with no success, and so I come to you on the advice of my chief priest. Only you can help, O great Goddess. Please be merciful to me, I have no other shelter."

Maha-Lakshmi replied "O dutiful prince, your noble desire can be fulfilled by that pure *brahmana*, Siddha-Samadhi. He lives by the gate of my temple. Go to him."

The prince gratefully took his leave and went directly to the residence of Siddha-Samadhi.

Falling at the feet of that great soul, the prince poured out his heart and begged for help. Siddha-Samadhi agreed and they both made haste to where the King's body laid preserved in a tub of pure boiled oil. Siddha-Samadhi chanted sacred prayers, and then sprinkled holy water over the head of the king.

The king immediately sat up. Dripping with oil and with a surprised expression on his face, the king inquired from the *brahmana*, "O great devotee, who are you?"

The prince then explained to his father all the events that had taken place. Having been saved from death, the king was most jubilant and grateful. He repeatedly bowed down at the feet of that pure *brahmana*.

The king asked, "How have you come to be blessed which such power?"

Siddha-Samadhi replied, "Every day I chant the twelfth chapter of *Bhagavad-gita*."

By the mercy of that great devotee, Siddha Samadhi, the king and his son also learned the twelfth chapter of *Bhagavad-gita* and in that way perfected their lives and retuned home to the spiritual world where they engaged in the eternal service of Lord Krishna.

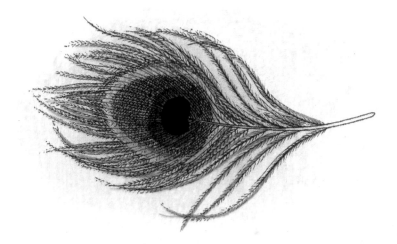

Chapter 12
Text 15

yasman nodvijate loko
lokan nodvijate ca yah
harsamarsa-bhayodvegair
mukto yah sa ca me priyah

He for whom no one is put into
difficulty and who is not disturbed
by anyone, who is balanced in
happiness and distress, fear and
anxiety, is very dear to Me.

The Tiger's Story

Lord Shiva said "Dear Parvati, please hear a glorious story in relation to the thirteenth chapter of *Bhagavad-gita*. I know it will bring joy to your heart."

Upon the banks of the Tungabhadra River in the South, there is an enchanting town called Hariharpur. The town is named after Lord Shiva, who is known as Harihar. He resides there in his deity form and grants benedictions to all who visit him.

In that town lived a learned *brahmana* who was well known for his simple, strict life-style. He had a wife who was the opposite to himself. The local people referred to her as Durachara, which means badly behaved. She mistreated her husband and spoke sharply to him with bad language. She behaved in the same manner towards her husband's friends. Durachara preferred to spend her time getting drunk and visiting her many male lovers, but she was never satisfied. Because the population of the town was expanding, Durachara built a small meeting place in the forest where she could meet her lovers privately.

One night, burning with desire, Durachara went to the meeting place in the forest hoping to find one of her lovers. Not finding anyone, she desperately searched the forest paths hoping to find someone to get drunk with and satisfy her lust. After wandering for a long time she became totally exhausted both in mind and body. Her heart and head throbbed with pain and frustration because her lust was not satisfied. In this feeble condition she sat down on the bare ground and simply wept. Nearby, a hungry tiger was resting. Hearing the sound of crying, the tiger swiftly approached the place where Durachara was sitting. Durachara heard the approaching footsteps

and hoping that it was one of her lovers, she eagerly rose up ready for an embrace, but to her sheer horror, from the shadows appeared the menacing form of a hungry tiger. She trembled in fear at the sight of his cruel eyes, sharp teeth and deadly claws.

Before the animal could pounce, she cried out "O tiger, before you rip me apart, please tell me who you are and why you are here?"

The tiger paused to consider the request and informed her, "By good fortune I can remember my previous birth and can understand the law of *karma*, therefore I do not devour devotees, *sannyasis* or chaste women. But you, O lusty woman, are most unchaste and will certainly be my food. However, first I will tell you my story as you have requested."

"Although I previously took birth in a *brahmana* family I had no good qualities. I was uncontrolled, mean and greedy. Sitting on the riverbank I would perform sacrifices and religious rites simply for money, which I hoarded and used for selfish purposes. I was interested only in my own pleasures and never gave in charity to those who were needy."

"Over the course of time, old age advanced on me, causing my eyesight to fail, my teeth to fall out and my hair to turn white but I still continued to unnecessarily collect more and more money. One day I made the mistake of visiting the house of some so-called *brahmanas* who were of bad character and cruel enough to set their dogs on me. One of those vicious dogs bit my leg very hard, causing me to fall on the ground, leaving me unable to move. Without receiving any help I died very quickly and for my sins received this tiger's body that you see before you now. That is my story, O wicked woman, and now I shall have you for lunch." He then devoured her.

The agents of death dragged away the soul of Durachara and threw her into a terrible hell. She was forced into a foul smelling swamp. She suffered there for millions of years. Then she was thrown into another hell called Raurava

74

where she suffered intolerable pain for many ages. She then took human birth on earth as a female dog-eater and again carried on with her sinful activities. Due to bad fortune she caught leprosy and tuberculosis. However, due to some good karma, she was fortunate to visit the holy place of Hariharpur. Nearby to the temple of Lord Shiva's consort, the Goddess Parvati, Durachara heard sacred recitations from the mouth of the great saint Vasudeva. He chanted the thirteenth chapter of *Bhagavad-gita* constantly. By hearing these recitations again and again she became free from all her sins, attained a divine four-armed form and entered into Vaikuntha. In this way, she perfected her life. Jai Shri Krishna!

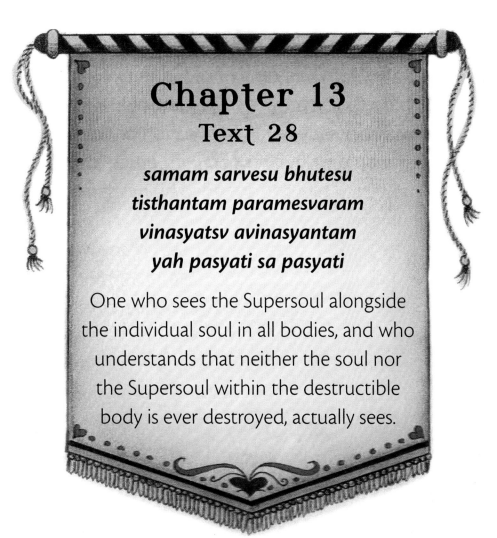

Chapter 13
Text 28

samam sarvesu bhutesu
tisthantam paramesvaram
vinasyatsv avinasyantam
yah pasyati sa pasyati

One who sees the Supersoul alongside the individual soul in all bodies, and who understands that neither the soul nor the Supersoul within the destructible body is ever destroyed, actually sees.

The Dog and the Rabbit

King Vikram-Betal ruled over an area of land called Simhaldvip. One day he decided to go hunting. He gathered together his son and two favourite hunting dogs. They galloped off towards the forest. Upon reaching the trees on the forest's edge, he spotted a wild rabbit, so he immediately released one of the dogs. The dog sped after the rabbit and a chase began with the king and his son in hot pursuit.

After much running, the chase finally slowed down as they reached a beautiful hermitage. The entire atmosphere of

that place was very peaceful. Deer were contentedly grazing in the shade of the fruit trees, while cheeky monkeys were jumping in the branches eating the fruits. Baby elephants were playing with tiger cubs in the grass and snakes were slithering closely among the proud peacocks, not caring that those birds were normally their deadly enemies. In the midst of this scene a resident *brahmana* of the hermitage had just finished washing his feet, leaving the earth in that spot wet and muddy. At that time, something wonderful happened.

The running rabbit and the pursuing hunting dog both slipped in the wet mud, and immediately attained divine bodies. At the same time, a glowing aerial chariot descended and swiftly took them up to the heavenly regions. The king witnessing all this was amazed and approached the *brahmana*, who being highly amused by those events, was laughing heartily.

Smiling, the king asked "Dear *brahmana*, I have never before seen such an incredible thing. As you appear to know something, please enlighten me."

"Yes, it is all very wonderful," replied the *brahmana*. "I will explain to you the cause of the rabbit and the dog ascending into heaven before our very eyes." The *brahmana* continued. "In the forest lives a great sage of the name Vatsa and he taught me to be always engaged in chanting the fourteenth chapter of the *Bhagavad-gita*. I was chanting those immortal words of Lord Krishna while washing my feet, and His power obviously entered into that water, consequently releasing both the rabbit and dog from their earthly forms. That in itself should be of no surprise, but now I will tell you why I was laughing."

"In Maharastra there is a town called Pratudhak and living there was a so-called *brahmana* by the name of Keshava. He was very cruel and had a wife called Vilobana. She had no self-control and enjoyed the company of many men. For this reason her husband became mad with rage and brutally killed her. Because of their sinful activities, in their next lives Keshava became that rabbit and Vilobana became the dog."

After hearing this wonderful narration, King Vikram-Betal was so inspired that he took up the daily recitation of the fourteenth chapter of the *Bhagavad-gita*. Upon leaving his body, he assumed a spiritual form and went to Vaikuntha where he engaged in the eternal service of Lord Krishna.

Chapter 14
Text 6

tatra sattvam nirmalatvat
prakasakam anamayam
sukha-sangena badhnati
jnana-sangena canagha

O sinless one, the path of goodness
being purer than the others, is
illuminating, and it frees one from
the results of sins. Those situated
on that path become filled with
happiness and knowledge.

The Commander Becomes a Horse

Lord Shiva said "Dear Parvarti, please listen with an attentive ear to the fifteenth chapter of *Bhagavad-gita* which is most glorious".

In the land of Gaudadesa there ruled a great king by the name of Narasimha. The head of the king's powerful army was called Sarab-Merunda, who planned with the prince to kill the king and take control of Gaudadesa. However, before that could happen, Sarab-Merunda died of cholera and took his birth in the land of Sindhu as a beautiful, fast-running horse.

One day, a successful young businessman from Gaudadesa spotted that fine horse and paid the owner a large sum of money for it. He immediately returned to Gaudadesa and presented it to King Narasimha. The king was most pleased with that magnificent horse and paid the businessman his asking price without so much as a second thought.

A few days later, the king mounted that horse and led a hunting party out to the forest. Seeing a deer in the distance, he immediately gave chase following the animal in every direction. Chasing over streams and through forests, he left his party behind, but still he could not catch the fleet-footed deer.

Eventually, exhaustion and thirst overtook the king, forcing him to dismount and take rest. He tied his mount to a tree and relaxed on a large rock. As he surveyed his surroundings, King Narasimha noticed a piece of parchment floating here and there in the breeze and as if by destiny, it landed beside him on the rock. "What's this?" he thought. Upon the parchment was written half a *shloka* of the fifteenth chapter of the *Bhagavad-gita*. The king read out loud those immortal words, and as he

spoke, his horse collapsed dead to the ground and from its body arose a divine four-armed being.

A flower-airplane from Vaikuntha appeared at the same time and transported that person away up into the sky. The monarch was astonished and felt himself truly blessed to have such an amazing vision. He stood up, looked around and noticed that not far away were many fruit trees surrounding an enchanting *ashram*. Approaching that place he saw a pure, self-controlled *brahmana* sitting and smiling. He went before that *brahmana* and with palms pressed together humbly and spoke to him.

"Dear *brahmana*, please will you explain everything to me?"

The *brahmana*, whose name was Vishnusharma, was pleased with the king's humble attitude and so replied, 'O King, previously you had in charge of your army a commander-in-chief by the name Sarab-Merunda. He plotted with your son to take away your kingdom.'

"However, he died of cholera before his plans could take place. He then took birth as that horse you rode and by good fortune heard the divine words you spoke from the fifteenth chapter of *Bhagavad-gita*, and thus he attained Vaikuntha."

Greatly inspired by this wonderful answer the king thankfully touched the parchment scroll to his head and took his leave. He joined up with the hunting party and joyfully returned to his palace. He felt the parchment scroll to be his greatest gain and repeatedly read what was written on it day after day. To fulfil the desire of his son, the king installed him as the ruler of Gaudadesa and retired to the forest where he attained the lotus feet of Lord Krishna by constantly reciting the fifteenth chapter of the *Bhagavad-gita*.

Chapter 15
Text 6

na tad bhasayate suryo
na sasanko na pavakah
yad gatva na nivartante
tad dhama paramam mama

That supreme abode of Mine is not
illumined by the sun or moon, nor by
fire or electricity.
Those who reach it never return
to this material world.

The King and the Elephant

Lord Shiva said "Dear Parvati, please hear from me one of the many glories of the sixteenth chapter of *Bhagavad-gita*."

Long, long ago, Maharaj Khadgabahu ruled over the rich and famous kingdom of Surat. Amongst his elephants was Arimardana, an extremely proud and passionate male who could not be easily approached. One day, seized by pride, frustration and anger, Arimardana broke free from his chains and ran wild in the city destroying everything in his path. The terrified citizens fled in all directions to escape his anger. The elephant keepers immediately informed the king of the bad news. The king quickly ran to the panic-filled scene to see what could be done. Things did not look good!

At that time, King Khadgabahu's eyes fell upon a peaceful *brahmana* from a distance. People were warning the *brahmana* of the danger ahead but he was not disturbed in any way. The *brahmana* was quietly chanting the first three verses of the sixteenth chapter of the *Bhagavad-gita*, which begins with the word *abhayam*, meaning fearlessness. He then calmly walked right up to the fearsome elephant and gently stroked him.

Touched by that pure *brahmana* the elephant became completely peaceful and lay down at his feet. The *brahmana* kindly patted the elephant and went on his way. Needless to say, the king and the citizens were totally amazed.

Regarding what they had just seen, no one could believe their eyes. Before the *brahmana* disappeared, the king quickly approached him, and after falling at his feet begged, "How have you acquired such amazing powers. Please tell me?"

The *brahmana* replied, "Everyday I chant some verses from the sixteenth chapter of *Bhagavad gita*."

"Dear brahmana," the king requested, "Please come to the palace and teach me those verses. This will be a great blessing for me."

That great-minded *brahmana* did as he was requested and received from the king the sum of one hundred gold coins.

The king recited those verses day after day until he became completely fearless, at which point he called for his guard who took him to where the dangerous elephant was kept. "Release him!" he ordered the elephant keepers. The citizens sent up a great cry, expecting chaos and destruction as before, but before that could happen, the king approached the released elephant and gently stroked him. The animal immediately lay down, just as it did with the *brahmana*, and as before everyone was astonished.

Satisfied by this, the king returned to his palace and installed the prince on the throne as his successor. Being freed from his responsibilities, King Khadgabahu peacefully retired to the forest to focus his attention on the chanting of the verses from the sixteenth chapter of *Bhagavad-gita*. In this way he perfected his human life by satisfying the Supreme Personality of Godhead, Lord Shri Krishna.

Any person who sincerely recites the sixteenth chapter of the *Bhagavad-gita*, regardless of any sinful acts he may have performed in the past, will certainly achieve the same result as Khadgabahu – the lotus feet of Lord Krishna.

Dushasan Becomes an Elephant

Lord Shiva continued "My dear Parvati, you have attentively heard some of the divine glories of the sixteenth chapter of *Bhagavad-gita* which features the great devotee, King Khadgabahu. Now please hear the glories of the seventeenth chapter, which also speaks of that same King".

This story is in connection with his life before he gave up his kingdom to go to the forest. It is told in the following way:

King Khadgabhu's son had many servants, one of which was extremely stupid and went by the name of Dushasan. Dushasan was so foolish, that he bet the prince he could mount and ride the most dangerous of all the royal elephants. The people begged him not to perform such a reckless act for he would surely die. Disregarding the good advice of his well-wishers, that foolish man climbed upon the back of the huge beast and urged him forward with strong words.

Having no tolerance for this, the proud and powerful elephant twisted and turned and ran wildly in all directions. In a matter of moments Dushasan was hurled to the ground and promptly stamped to death by that enraged beast. The law of *karma* rules that whatever one's mind is fixed upon at the time of death, that is what one gets without fail. As such, in his next life, Dushasan was born as an elephant and lived in the palace of the King of Simhaldwip.

Now it so happened that this king was a close friend of King Khadgabahu, and they often exchanged gifts. On one occasion the King of Simhaldwip sent his friend that elephant as a gift. King Khadgabahu in turn gave it to his favourite poet. Some time later the poet sold the elephant to the King of Malva for one hundred gold coins.

The elephant lived happily for some time but then became seriously ill and was unable to eat or drink. The elephant keepers tried everything in their power to make the animal well but failed in their attempts, so they reported the bad news to the king. The king of Malva immediately called

for the very best doctors and went to the stricken elephant. A very wonderful thing then happened. To the utter amazement of all the people present, the dying elephant spoke to the king in a grave voice. "My dear king, you are the best of men and a follower of the laws of *dharma*. You always engage in the worship of the Supreme God, Lord Vishnu, therefore who can compare with you? As for me, my time is drawing to an end and death is close by. Please understand that it is too late for medicines and doctors. Even giving in charity or the performance of sacrifices will be of no use. If you want to help me please do one thing. Bring to me someone who daily recites the seventeenth chapter of *Bhagavad-gita*."

Dutifully, the king found a great devotee who regularly chanted the seventeenth chapter of the *Bhagavad-gita*. While uttering those words, that devotee sprinkled holy water on the elephant's head and the elephant immediately gave up his body and received a divine four-armed form like that of Lord Vishnu. A flower-airplane came to take him away but before he left, the King of Malva asked him to explain everything. Dushasan told him all about his previous life and how he had received an elephants body. Then he left for Vaikuntha.

The king was so inspired by these events he took up the recitation of the seventeenth chapter of the *Bhagavad-gita* and perfected his life by attaining the lotus feet of Lord Krishna.

Chapter 17
Text 4

yajante sattvika devan
yaksa-raksamsi rajasah
pretan bhuta-ganams canye
yajante tamasa janah

Those in goodness worship the
demigods; the greedy worship the
demons; and those in ignorance
worship ghosts and spirits.

The New Indra

Parvati said "My dear husband, having heard from you the glories of the seventeenth chapter of *Bhagavad-gita* I am now most eager to hear the glories of the eighteenth and final chapter of that wonderful narration."

Lord Shiva replied "My dear wife, please hear from me the glories of the eighteenth chapter of *Bhagavad-gita* which can offer unlimited bliss to the faithful devotee and purify the heart of all material desires. It is the essence of Lord Krishna, whose divine words give life and inspiration to demigods such as Lord Indra, and famous *yogis* like Sanak and Sananda.

One day, the king of heaven Lord Indra, was sitting peacefully on his throne with his wife Sachi. The demigods were nicely serving him when something extraordinary happened. A beautiful young person, followed by servants of Lord Vishnu, arrived in the palace and quickly walked up to Indra's throne. Suddenly, Indra fainted and fell to the floor for a few moments. On opening his eyes he saw that the new arrival had ascended his throne. The demigods then took the crown that had fallen from Indra's head and placed it on the head of the new arrival. The demigods and other noble members of the heavenly realm gathered around the new Indra and glorified him with many words. Rites were performed and offerings were made, with many *rishis* coming forward, chanting Vedic mantras. They offered their blessings to the new Indra. Then heavenly performers, known as *gandharvas* and *apsaras* sang and played beautiful music. They performed wonderful dancing for the pleasure of the new Indra, who beamed smiles in all directions.

The displaced Indra picked himself up and stepped away from the scene in a state of shock. He thought deeply about what he had seen. "Normally, a new Lord Indra gains his position by performing one hundred horse sacrifices, but this new person, as far as I know, has performed none, yet still he is enjoying all the benefits of the king of heaven. How can this be?" Thinking in this way, he further pondered, "This person has never performed great acts of charity in holy places or fed the masses. To my knowledge, he has never created ponds, dug wells or planted trees for the benefit of the people. So how, in heavens name, could he have earned the right to take over my position? This cannot be right."

Greatly disturbed at heart, the usurped Indra travelled to the Ocean of Milk and prayed for the *darshan* of Lord Vishnu. After some time had passed, Lord Vishnu granted him audience.

"My dear Lord Vishnu" he begged, "You know everything and are very kind to Your devotees, therefore please relieve my distress. A new person has taken over my throne, yet I am convinced he has not fulfilled the normal requirements for becoming king of heaven. Please explain everything to me, for I am most disturbed."

Lord Vishnu smiled and said, "My dear Indra, you should not be surprised. The devotee who has taken your position chanted five verses from the eighteenth chapter of the *Bhagavad-gita* throughout his entire life, and because of that, has achieved the rewards normally earned by all sorts of welfare activities and sacrifices. Not only will he enjoy being king of heaven for many years, but also in his next life, he will join me forever in the spiritual realm. You too can achieve this divine destination simply by the constant recitation of the eighteenth chapter of *Bhagavad-gita*."

Hearing these wonderful instructions, all grief left the heart of Indra, and he became fully joyful. With strong determination he took his leave of Lord

Vishnu, transformed himself into a *brahmana* and made his way to the town of Kalegrani on the bank of the Godavari River. Near that place, on the bank of the river, a saintly person was sitting and reciting the verses of the eighteenth chapter of *Bhagavad-gita*. By chanting those verses everyday, he had understood the goal of all Vedic knowledge, and was thus perfectly satisfied within himself. Upon seeing that saint, Indra immediately fell at his feet and humbly begged him to teach him those very same verses. Being very merciful, the saint did as he was requested.

Indra perfected his life by chanting those holy verses and achieved the divine destination of Vishnuloka. In that eternal abode he experienced all varieties of bliss in the service of the Lord, considering the pleasures of heaven to be no more than dry straw blowing in the wind.

Lord Shiva continued, "My dear Parvati, the eighteenth chapter of *Bhagavad-gita* is especially powerful and by chanting its verses, with full attention, the great sages easily attain the ultimate perfection of life, Lord Krishna's lotus feet. Not only that, but any person who attentively studies these stories that I have narrated to you, will be relieved of all their sins. By remembering these stories with great faith a person will, in due course of time, enjoy all the pleasures of heaven and at the end of their mortal life, enter into Vaikuntha, the spiritual world."

So concludes the Gita-Mahatmya which was spoken by Lord Shiva to his wife Parvati Devi.

GOVINDA

Chapter 18
Text 66

sarva-dharman parityajya
mam ekam saranam vraja
aham tvam sarva-papebhyo
moksayisyami ma sucah

Abandon all varieties of religion
and just surrender unto Me.
I shall deliver you from all sinful
reactions. Do not fear.

Ananṭa Shakṭi Das

After completing a 3 year course at the Bournemouth & Poole College of Arts, UK he joined the Hare Krishna Movement and took commissions to design and construct altars, backdrops and murals in Mauritius and South Africa.

Since returning to England in 1982 he has specialised in religious paintings alongside writing and illustrating educational books based on Indian classics. He now resides in Hertfordshire, UK.

Other books he has worked on are:

Vedic Stories from Ancient India
Vaishnava Saints
Creation - A Story from India
Mahabharata
The Life of Ramanujacharya
Shri Pushpanjali
Passage from India
Pancha Tantra
Krishna Story Book